THE PALACE
OF THE HUNGARIAN
ACADEMY
OF SCIENCES

GYÖRGY RÓZSA

THE PALACE
OF THE HUNGARIAN
ACADEMY
OF SCIENCES

BUDAPEST · 1984

LIBRARY OF THE HUNGARIAN ACADEMY OF SCIENCES

ISBN 963 7301 534

CONTENTS

I. THE HISTORY
OF THE PALACE'S DESIGN
AND CONSTRUCTION

"The beautiful palace of the Academy has a dual significance for us: on the one hand, it is the most successful building of our capital constructed in the third quarter of the 19th century; on the other, it is the earliest member of the long row of palaces which transformed Budapest, once humble and provincial, into one of the most beautiful cities of our age," said Károly Pulszky, the eminent art historian whose words of 1892 can still be applied to determine the standing of the palace in the architectural history and the townscape of Budapest. It is, therefore, worthwhile to provide for the guidance of today's visitor a description of the building and a short summary of the circumstances of its origin.

The supreme governing body of Hungary's scientific life, the Academy of Sciences, was established in 1825, on public initiative. During the first forty years of its existence it had no permanent home of its own. At the beginning it resided on the first floor of the Deron-, later Nákó-house which once occupied the site of today's Gresham-palace in Roosevelt Square. Later, it moved to the first and second floors of the Trattner-Károlyi-house in No. 3, Petőfi Sándor Street. Sessions were held in the County Hall and, after its completion, in the Ceremonial Hall of the Hungarian National Museum.

It was only after the collapse of the 1848 Revolution, at the end of the 1850s, that conditions for the erection of an independent building were created for the Academy. The necessary funds were raised by the campaign relying on the national upsurge against absolutism. Then, as at the time of the foundation of the Academy, it was possible to move wide strata of society in support of Hungarian science. There were those who wanted to appropriate part of the new museum building for the purposes of the Academy, and others, who wanted to erect a new building on the corner of the museum site. Fortunately, both ideas were rejected and a decision was made to build an independent palace for the Academy. In 1859 Count Emil Dessewffy, the second president of the Academy, started a collection for the palace. He chose the site of the palace as well, on the busiest and one of the finest squares of the city at that time, on the Pest side bridge-head of the Chain Bridge. He was able to obtain the site on favourable terms partly as a donation of the city of Pest, partly as the result of an advantageous barter with the Dunagőzhajózási Társaság (Danube Steamship Co.). The Academy's Board of Directors nominated a three-member Building Committee consisting of, besides Count Dessewffy, vice-president Baron József Eötvös and Count György Károlyi, a friend of István Széchenyi and a founder member, too. In all matters of construction they were invested with full powers.

The committee, without inviting an open tender, called on Imre Henszlmann (1813—1888), an associate of the Academy and a historian of architecture, Heinrich Ferstel (1828—1893), the architect of the *Votivkirche* in Vienna, and Miklós Ybl (1814—1891) who already possessed considerable experience, to submit plans for the new building. Young Antal Skalnitzky (1836—1878), who had recently returned from Berlin, and Frigyes Feszl (1821—1884), the architect of the Redoute just under construction, submitted their designs without invitation. As the Building Committee was not satisfied with the designs received, Leo von Klenze (1784—1864) of Munich and Friedrich August Stüler (1806—1865), the architect of the Berlin *Nationalgalerie,* the *Neues Museum* and the Stockholm *Nationalmuseum*, were also invited to contribute.

The Building Committee's evaluation of the designs aroused great controversy. Architects, art historians, and laymen alike took part in the wide-ranging debate in the press to express their views. For the first time architecture became public concern in Hungary. The debate centred on the decision whether the neo-Gothic or neo-Renaissance trend of historism was more suitable for the design of a mid-19th century building destined to be the headquarters of an institution governing the country's scientific life. At the same time the debate aroused interest in the problems of Hungarian national architectural style.

Henszlmann, who cooperated with Károly Gerster (1819—1867) and Lajos Frey (1829—1877) supported by Arnold Ipolyi, as well as Ferstel and Feszl, represented the neo-Gothic trend, while the others were for the neo—Renaissance version. According to Henszlmann neo-Renaissance was "a deteriorated form of Greek style bequeathed upon us third-hand" lacking any national features. Incorrectly, he considered the characteristic style of Hungary's national past to be the Gothic style. Count János Waldstein, a friend of Széchenyi, put the opposition's views into words most succinctly: "There may be, and are, Gothic railway

8

stations, train terminals and watch-houses, as they convey no thought, but there cannot be Gothic Academies as they must convey ideas which are impossible to express through the Gothic style." After exhibiting the plans in the National Museum, their release and violent debate in the press, Budapest was enriched with its first monumental public building in the second half of the 19th century when the Building Committee accepted Stüler's plan, which undoubtedly was the most suitable, modified according to local requirements. Its clearness, the noble harmony of its proportions, and its perfect perspective made it one of the most prominent sights on the Danube embankment. Although the fact that the committee awarded the commission to a foreigner supported the view that Hungarian architects of the time were incapable of carrying out a task on this scale, nevertheless, it is also a fact that the wide-ranging debate and Stüler's work gave a new impulse to Hungarian architecture. Besides the aesthetic debate about the styles of earlier ages it would now be considered strange for a scholar, even if cooperating with practising architects, to participate in architectural design.

Károly Pulszky, already quoted earlier, formulated the concept of late eclecticism at the turn of the century: "Who doubts these days that any style is suitable for a monumental palace that can satisfy practical requirements; and who is not aware that all of them are as specifically Hungarian as not; that various architectural styles are not the private property of nations but the common heritage of modern culture to be drawn upon by all architects according to the demands of the tasks to be accomplished."

Construction work, supervised by Ybl and Skalnitzky on behalf of Stüler, lasted from April 1862 to 1865. For financial reasons, between 1863—1864 a block of flats was built at the back of the plot, designed by Ybl and supervised by József Diescher (about 1811—1874) who was site architect at the construction of the palace as well. Total expenditure, including the cost of the site and block of flats, amounted to 1 million florins. Although the weekly meetings were already held in the unfinished palace, formal inauguration took place only on December 11th, 1865. A medal by Karl Radnitzky of Vienna (1818—1901), an album by Ignác Schrecker, containing photographs of the 250 members of the Academy, and the "Memorial Volume for the Inauguration Ceremony of the Palace of the Hungarian Academy of Sciences" (Pest, 1865) preserve the memory of the ceremony.

At the time of the design of the palace its upper floors were already taken into consideration to accomodate the exhibits of the Esterházy Gallery, transferred to

9

Pest in trust. Although this was not related to the original function of a learned society, it provided a temporary solution for the showing of an art collection of basic cultural importance through the financial sacrifice of Hungarian society. The Gallery was opened on December 12th, 1865 in five rooms on the second, and nine rooms on the third floor of the palace. In 1871 the Hungarian state purchased the whole collection which became the foundation of today's Museum of Fine Arts under the name of Országos Képtár (National Gallery).

After a fire which broke out in the building on February 5, 1869, Ybl replaced the wooden roof with a steel construction. Between 1865 and 1876, until its own place was built on Népköztársaság Road (formerly Andrássy Road), the Art Society also operated in the building. After 1906, on completion of the Museum of Fine Arts, the vacant exhibition halls on the third floor of the Academy were assigned to house the Historical Picture Gallery, founded in 1884. It was open between 1907—1914 and from 1923 until the outbreak of World War II, when the collection was moved to the National Museum. Contemporary pictures of exhibitions of the Esterházy Gallery and of the Historical Picture Gallery are valuable documents showing the methods used to organize fine art exhibitions in the past.

In addition to the above institutions the palace housed, for varying periods, the committees of the Houses of Parliament, Benczúr's master class of painting (from 1883), the State Painting School for Women (from 1888), the Kisfaludy Society (from 1865), the Society of Natural Sciences, and the National Board for Architectural Monuments in the 1870s.

During World War II the building suffered severe damage. It was restored in several phases. Between 1948—49 the exterior and the ground floor premises, in 1950 the first floor and the Department of Manuscripts, in 1954 the frescoes of the Assembly Hall and in 1958 the second floor premises were restored. In 1963 external restoration became necessary again.

II. THE BUILDING

At the time of its construction, the Academy's evenly proportioned monumental block with its quadrangle was the most impressive building in one of the most important squares of the capital. The clear arrangement and harmonious division of its facade is still an important element in the townscape of the Danube embankment. This building in Budapest is one of Stüler's masterpieces in which he, a follower of the Classicist Schinkel and the last true representative of 19th century Prussian architecture, blended the elements of Hellenism and the Renaissance of northern Italy. The National Museum of Stockholm, with its narrower and lower projection and side wings with 6—6 axes, puts greater emphasis on the horizontal line. Its surface is much more serene than that of the more representative Budapest palace. In Stockholm, the classicist mass-effect of the building and its historical-style decorative motifs contrast with each other.

The width of the main facade facing Roosevelt Square is 58 metres, those of the facades facing Akadémia Street and the Danube are equally 51 metres. The height of the projection is 28 metres, that of the wings 22 metres. The projection containing the building's most important interior having a distinguished function, the Assembly Hall, is quintaxial and three storeys high. Above red marble steps, three of five arches nestle doors which lead into the building. The balustraded open balcony above the arches is accessible through the Assembly Hall. The middle projection is broken up by paired Corinthian columns, which, complying with the height of the Assembly Hall, join two floors together, while on the sides wall pilasters replace the columns. At the time of the palace's construction the columned projection corresponded to the Classicist central section with its columns and tympanum of the Lloyd Palace, which enclosed the Square from the South. The lower section of the shafts of the fluted columns and pillars are adorned with grotesque carvings; the capitals are decorated with half-figures. The coat of arms of Hungary containing the crown is supported by angels floating

11

above the central window. This and the genius above the other windows is the work of Miklós Izsó (1831—1875), an outstanding Hungarian sculptor of the 19th century. The inscriptions above the windows are the following: HAZAFIAK ALA-PÍTOTTÁK [Founded by Patriots] / MDCCCXXV — MŰKÖDNI KEZDETT [Commenced Operation] / MDCCCXXXI — NEMZETI RÉSZVÉT EMELTE [Raised by the Nation] / MDCCCLX — HÁZA FELÉPÜLT [Its Palace Completed] / MDCCCLXIV. A frieze inscribed with „MAGYAR TUDOMÁNYOS AKADÉ-MIA" [Hungarian Academy of Sciences] and a cornice tops the main floor and supports the paired Corinthian columns and wall pilasters of the upper floor. These are smaller and less richly decorated. There are statues in the intercolumnia-tions and the space above them is decorated with terracotta Apollon and Minerva heads set in medallions. The attic crown mould above the three-sectional main beam is supported by helical corbels. The projection is topped by an attic with baluster railing and sturdy pilasters. Once terracotta sphinxes stood at its cor-ners but they had to be removed later because of damage. The side walls of the projection contain round-arched windows on ground level alone, otherwise only the terracotta frieze, running on from the facade between the Corinthian wall pilasters and their capitals, brightens up their surface. The facades of the quart-axial wings are only two storeys high, and much simpler than the projection. With the exception of the cellar windows, all the other windows are round-arched, arranged in pairs on the upper floors. The effect of the larger windows of the main floor alternating with Corinthian wall pilasters is emphasized by baluster railings continuing the balustraded balcony of the projection. The balustered attic also extends towards the wings but, in contrast to the projection at second floor level. On ground level the wings end in a rusticated wall pilaster which extends towards the first floor into a Tuscan wall pilaster framed with lath. On the two sides of the second floor stand the terracotta statues of Galilei and Miklós Révai the linguist, while above the attic the corners are brought into prominence by candelabra. The finish of the crown mould is similar to that of the projection.

*

The simpler Akadémia Street facade has 15 axes, in the ninth of which from the left is a gate. Besides the cornice, the wall surface is broken up alternately by round-arched windows and Corinthian wall pilasters. Under the first floor windows the baluster railing of the main facade continues. The ground floor windows are lower than those of the main facade; above them open the small square windows of the service flats of the mezzanine. The second floor windows are also paired. The statues of Descartes and Leibniz stand at the corners.

The facade facing the Danube has 13 axes. The three larger central windows, positioned corresponding to the conference room for weekly sessions are accentuated by four rusticated wall pilasters. On the second floor there are statues above the columns. The windows of the side facades alternate   with Corinthian wall pilasters on both floors. The first floor windows are also decorated with a row of balusters. The balustered attic with candelabra at its corners appears here, too, like on the Akadémia Street facade. The terracotta statues of Newton and Raffaello stood at the second floor corners, but the latter, damaged during World War II, had to be replaced with the statue of Lomonosov by Gyula Palotai (1911—1976).

*

The allegorical figures representing the sciences on the second floor of the Danube side facade and on the third floor of the main facade are the following, from left to right: Archaeologia, Poesis, Cosmographia, Politica — Jurisprudentia, Historia, Physiographia, Mathematica, Philosophia and Philologia (Archaeology, Poetry, Geography, Politics — Jurisprudence, History, Natural Sciences, Mathematics, Philosophy, Philology). Of the original statues that of Miklós Révai was carved by Miklós Izsó; the rest by the Ernst March Co. of Charlottenburg of terracotta using the models produced by Emil Wolf (1802—1879), a student of Thorwaldsen, and other German sculptors. The allegorical statues and ornamental details of the facades are replicas, some used to decorate other buildings as well. The palace was built of brick, only the facade is stonework. The pedestal was made of Hungarian red marble, the ornaments of Siklós and Bükkösd marble. Besides clerks of works József Diescher and Izsó, the following Hungarian masters took part in the masonry work and the marble cutting: László Halász (about 1820 — about 1882), János Marschalkó (1819—1877), János Kauser (1817—?), Antal Gerenday (1818—1887), Lajos Hofhauser, Vencel Szlavek, József Kehlendorfer, I. Vogl, and Opnich, the stone mason of Trieste.

*

The memorial tablet commemorating the scene of the foundation of the Academy was placed   at the Roosevelt Square end of the Akadémia Street facade. It was the work of Barnabás Holló (1866–1917), an outstanding figure of Hungarian sculpture. The idea of a memorial tablet first emerged in 1884 but it was only on February 15th 1891, that Baron Lóránd Eötvös made a definite proposal. The two-metre high, five-metre wide tablet, cast by the Beschorner Co. for 11,000 Florins, was unveiled on January 15th, 1893.

Although Vinzenz Katzler's (1823–1882) lithograph, illustrating László Kotsányi's Széchenyi biography published in 1860 stood at his disposal as a model, Barnabás Holló could easily surpass its artistic qualities. The long table, dividing the composition horizontally into two parts, stands in a Rococo-style hall. On the right two arched openings command a view of Pozsony castle, recalling the scene of the National Assembly. The artist modelled the features of individual participants using, as far as possible, authentic sources. Slightly right of centre, at the side of the table towards the viewer, stands Széchenyi in his Hussar officer's uniform, as he offers his income for a year for the purposes of the Academy.

Miklós Kolozsváry and István Szoboszlai Pap, Calvinist pastor, stand on the left-hand side, between them the head of János Balogh, the Member for the County of Bars, is visible. István Máriássy, the Member for the County of Gömör and chairman of the regional session, sits at the head of the table, Gábor Döbrentei, Gáspár Takács and György Bartal, Members for Pozsony, stand behind him. Pál Felsőbüki Nagy, Member for Sopron, sits on the near side of the table with his back to the viewer. His words, just pronounced, still keep the audience in suspense. On the far side of the table, between the sitting figure of Pál Nagy and the standing figure of Széchenyi, Count József Dessewffy, Deputy for Szabolcs county, Count György Andrássy, Deputy for Torna, and Baron Ábrahám Vay, the Deputy for Borsod, are seated. The prominent place of the latter two men was apparently due to their sizeable donations which immediately followed Széchenyi's. Behind Széchenyi, Mihály Platthy, Member for Bars, and keeper of minutes sits on the far side of the table. Count György Károlyi dominates the right-hand side group, also owing to his substantial donation. Besides him, Mihály Esterházy and Zsigmond Perényi, Members for Bereg, are standing, while Miklós Wesselényi's sitting figure effectively completes the clear-cut, successful composition, an outstanding work of Hungarian historical relief sculpture and worthy commemoration of a great event.

III. THE GROUND FLOOR

Through the main gate we enter a vestibule divided into three aisles by four pairs of columns on each side and separated from the corridor which connects the longitudinal wings seven steps higher, by three arched openings. On the walls of the vestibule marble pilasters correspond to the columns. Their base, similarly to the lower part of the rails that divide the corridor, is of imitation marble. The archivolts and the cross-ribs are decorated with stucco reliefs of braided-pattern. Besides the masters already mentioned, the flooring and the artificial marmoration is the work of Odorico Odorico of Vienna and the Rojcsek brothers of Pest. The vestibule was the scene of ceremonial funerals on several occasions. Among others, laid out in state here, were Ferenc Deák, the statesman (1876), János Arany, the poet and secretary general of the Academy (1882), Pál Gyulai, the historian of literature (1909), Kálmán Mikszáth, the great novelist (1910), and Zoltán Kodály, the composer (1967).

From the vestibule a cross corridor divided by a white marble baluster railing leads to the premises of the Library of the Academy, one of the oldest and greatest public libraries of the country, founded by József Teleki in 1826. Its present objective is twofold: on the one hand, by means of its holding and international connections it assists scientific research, on the other, it acts as a central library for the network of the libraries of the Academy's institutes. Its periodicals collection in the arts field is the most important in Hungary.

Turning to the left from the corridor, we enter a small antechamber where the statues of József Teleki and Ferenc Toldy, the secretary general and the first chief librarian, stand. The former is the work of István Ferenczy (1792–1856), and the latter of Alajos Stróbl (1856–1926). The catalogue room is decorated with the portraits of Pál Hunfalvy (by Róbert Wellmann, 1866–1946), Ferenc Toldy (a copy), Kálmán Szily (by Géza Biczó, 1853–1907), Ágost Heller (by Andor

Boruth, 1873–1955), and József Szinnyei (by Gyula Tury, 1866–1932). The portraits in the main reading room are the following: Sándor Kőrösi Csoma (a copy), János Batsányi (a copy), Farkas Bolyai (a copy), Boldizsár Elischer by Ede Balló (1859–1936) and István Széchenyi (a copy). The memorial tablet of the Teleki family is the work of János Marschalkó, that of György Ráth of the Gerenday Co.; the joint memorial tablet of Zsigmond Reiner, István Sándor, Tamás Siskovits, Andor Semsey and Ferenc Vigyázó was carved by Ernő Jálics (1895–1964). The portraits in the periodicals reading room are the following: Károly Bérczy and József Gaál, both by Ignác Roskovics (1854–1915), Móric Lukács by Bertalan Székely (1835–1910) and Sándor Győry by Ede Heinrich (1819–1885).

Turning to the right from the vestibule we come to the Oriental Collection of international reputation, opened in 1951. The valuable Manuscript Collection forming a joint department with the Collection of Old Books is located on the first floor; both are accessible through a flight of stairs from the courtyard. Of the paintings decorating its walls, we would mention the portrait of Bálint Balassi, copied by Géza Biczó from the contemporary original of the Bálint Balassi Museum in Esztergom.

Returning to the stately vestibule, from here, opposite the main entrance, we come to the staircase. In spite of the relatively limited space available, a solemn effect is nevertheless achieved by its successful exploitation. Antal Skalnitzky used the same design ten years later for the staircase of the University Library. The semicircular outer wall of the staircase extends towards the courtyard. The straight, lower section of the stairs, consisting of steps made of white karst marble, is lit through three semicircular arched windows. At mezzanine level the stairs branch off into two arched arms which lead up to the first floor. The landing is supported by Tuscan pillars. The marble bust of István Széchenyi, sculptured by László Dunaiszky (1822–1904) in 1877, was placed on the landing. The pilasters of the side walls and the red Verona-marble columns which support the arches of the semicircular openings are decorated with rosette- and Corinthian motifs. The pedestal of the staircase balustrade is made of artificial marble, and the railing itself of gold-plated cast iron, produced in the Schlick Works of Pest.

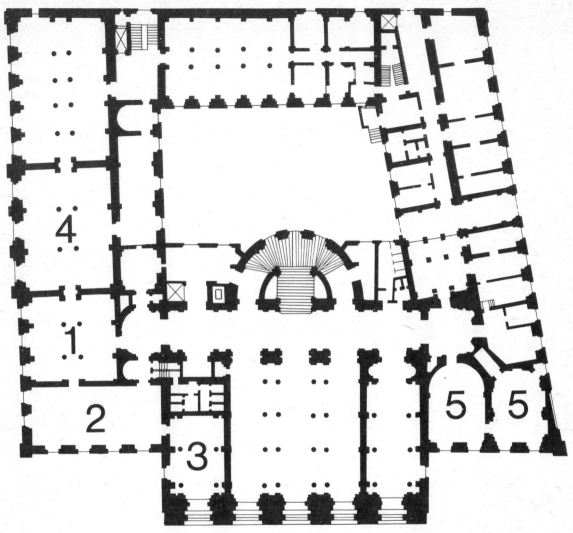

Ground floor plan
1. Catalogue Room. 2. Reading Room. 3. Periodicals Reading Room. 4. Stacks. 5. Oriental Collection.

IV. THE FIRST FLOOR

The arabesque-decorated archivolts of the first floor corridor are supported by fluted, paired Ionic columns. On the wall facing the stairs there are three niches. They are framed with paired columns of Pécs red marble and stand on a stucco plinth with pseudo-Corinthian pilasters behind them. The capitals of the pilasters are connected with an arabesque-adorned frieze; the spandrels of the niches contain plaster reliefs of candelabra and syrens. In the central niche stands the bust of János Arany, a plaster cast replica of the marble original by Miklós Izsó, held by the National Museum. On the left we see the marble bust of Stüler, the architect of the palace. Its erection had been decided on October 30th when news came of the master's death, and it has been carved by Miklós Izsó after the original of Hermann Schievelbein (1817—1867) of Berlin. The niche on the right holds the bust of Kálmán Mikszáth, sculptured by Barnabás Holló in 1910.

Between the niches two richly carved doors set in Renaissance-style plaster frames lead to the Assembly Hall. The mahogany wood used for the doors and the Assembly Hall panelling was donated by Károly László, a Hungarian citizen who emigrated to Mexico.

*

The two-storey high, 35-metre long and 17-metre wide *Assembly Hall* is the most impressive and stately interior of the palace. The fine Salzburg red marble has only been used for the columns supporting the galleries on the three sides. Some of the factory-processed details, made of cheaper material (such as the caryatides) were originally applied as a temporary measure for the sake of economy but they remained and interfere with the general effect of the hall. The canvas-lined plaster statues, modelled on Berlin originals, were cast by János Marschalkó, already mentioned several times before. As the hall was primarily meant for daytime use, the platform was originally situated in front of the windows. A carpet was embroidered for it in 75 x 75 cm squares by "patriotic women" at the appeal of Mrs. János Bohus, eye witness of the surrender at Világos, after the 1848 Revolution.

The idea to decorate the walls of the Assembly Hall with frescoes emerged quite early. President József Eötvös said in his inauguration speech: "When science marches victorious into her palace given to her as a gift by the entire nation, let it be opened to the domestic fine arts as well. A nobler ground for devoting all its energies cannot offer itself than the decoration of the Academy, and for the nation, no better chance for the support of domestic artists than the provision of this opportunity."

The committee to formulate the programme of the frescoes comprised József Eötvös, Ágoston Trefort, Mihály Horváth, Arnold Ipolyi and Vilmos Fraknói, i.e. all the scholars, writers and politicians who strove for the development of Hungarian historical painting. The drafting of the programme was Arnold Ipolyi's work. Originally, they wanted to commission Mihály Munkácsy (1844–1900), Gyula Benczúr (1844–1920) and Sándor Liezenmayer (1839–1898) who was studying in Munich, to do the painting, but none of them were able to find the time. Eventually, the frescoes of the Assembly Hall were painted by Károly Lotz (1833–1904), one of the leading masters of Hungarian monumental painting. A collection was taken up to secure the financial basis. The paintings, using the *al secco* technique, were framed by gold-plated plaster decorations, designed by architect Albert Schickedanz (1846–1915), artistic designer of Heroes' Square, and executed by Adolf Götz, a teacher of the school of technical drawing. The paintings were prepared in three phases: the allegories of the ceiling in 1887, the triptych on the Danube-side wall in 1887–1888, and the one opposite in 1891. For the wall facing the windows and originally the platform, therefore the main wall, mural painting was designed depicting figures of Hungary's post-Baroque literature like György Bessenyei, Széchenyi and Kossuth, but this was never executed. The fact, that the Citadel of Hungarian Science was decorated with wall paintings depicting literary history, was the outcome of the ruling school of thought at the time of the establishment of the Academy and throughout the 19th century, which saw the duty of the institution besides promoting scientific progress to develop the Hungarian language as well.

The wall-paintings on the shorter sidewalls are triptyches; the architectural design of their background unites the triple field divided by pillars into one. On

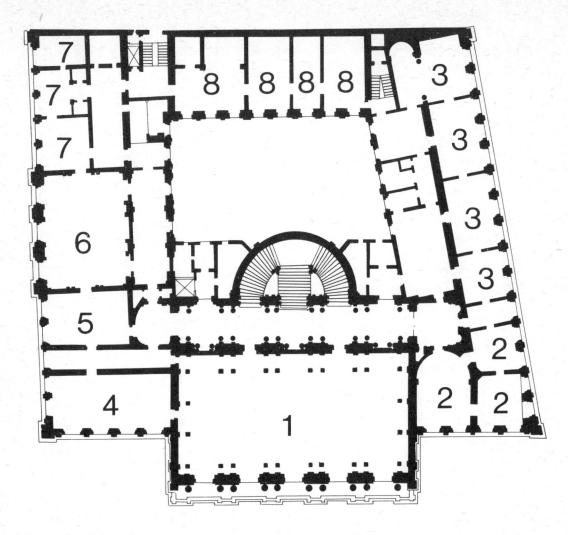

Ground plan of the first floor
1. Assembly Hall. 2. Presidium. 3. Scientists' Club. 4. Presidential Conference Room. 5. Hall of Pictures. 6. Lecture Hall. 7. Secretary General's Office. 8. Collection of Manuscripts and Old Books.

the Danube side, a structure resembling the apse of a Romanesque church is the common background for the paintings representing the age when Saint Stephen, Coloman Beauclerc, and Louis the Great were reigning in Hungary. Because of his prominent position, King Stephen, standing in front of the spiral-columned, Romanesque tabernacle, becomes the main figure of all three compositions. He wears a purple robe, the realistically represented Hungarian royal crown adorns his head and the coronation cloak his shoulder. With his left he points at the apostolic cross and extends his right towards Prince Imre who kneels in front of him in a scarlet dolman and a blue-lined white cloak, and holds the Scroll of Admonitions written by Stephen. Gellért stands next to Imre in his bishop's vestments; masters Walter and Henrik of Pannonhalma appear on the left in the foreground. Hartvik, King Stephen's biographer, stands in the background to the left, next to a youth. In the centre of the foreground, leaning against a Romanesque baptismal font, there is a slab with the inscription: "EMLÉKEZZÜNK RÉGIEKRE!" [Remember the Ancients!]

To the right of the king a monk in a brown gown holds high the apostolic cross, behind him an architect-friar presents the model of the Székesfehérvár cathedral. On the right a grey-haired monk instructs a boy and a girl, behind them appears the hooded head of a violinist.

In the left-hand side picture the central figure is Coloman Beauclerk who protests against the witch-burning imminent on the left of the foreground, by pointing at the code of laws in his right hand. His dolman is yellow, he wears a blue cloak lined with lilac-coloured material on his shoulder, and a strip-crown with cross on his head. To the right in the foreground a minstrel breaking his lute and a warrior with his sword lowered recalls the defeat of pagan culture. Behind them rise the figures of Saint Margaret and master Rogerius, the author of *Carmen Miserabile* which records the Mongol invasion. On the left Pelbárt Temesvári preaches from the pulpit while the background is populated with figures, both secular and clerical.

The right-hand side picture leads the observer to the era of Louis I. The king stands level with King Coloman at the top of the painted steps in yellow dolman and blue cloak, and studies the model of Pécs University presented to him by the architect. The fine arts of the period are evoked by a model of Saint Ladislaus' statue of Nagyvárad and the figure of a fresco painter working in the background. The figures dressed in Oriental garments, standing on the painted gallery, depict the characters of medieval mystery plays. The bearded figure of the valiant Mik-

22

lós Toldi, attired in red, rises above the King's retinue. An old peasant on the right-hand side of the painting is its conceptual centre. The group of clerics listening to his story consists of Anonymus the chronicler, Thomas the archdeacon of Spalato, and János Thuróczy, the historian. On the left, in the foreground, stands, in the company of one of his fellow monks, the Dominican Friar Julian, discoverer of the Hungarians who had remained in their country of origin.

The triptych on the opposite wall summarizes the Renaissance and Baroque centuries. Its unity of form is assured by the painted structure of the galleried, open-centred Renaissance hall. The central painting acquires an independent background by book-shelves referring to Matthias Corvinus' world-famous library the *Corvina*, screened off by a green curtain, with the busts of Homer and Julius Caesar placed on their top bracket.

In the still life of the foreground, alongside the books and a printing press, natural science also makes its appearance, represented by a globe. The back of the king's high throne is decorated with the Erdődy-tapestry, a valuable relic of the textile arts of the 15th century. The monarch is dressed in a goldbrocade dolman and a blue velvet cloak. The Italian members of his court stand to his right: Filippo Lippi holding a painting of the Madonna, a group of historians with Luigi Carbo of Ferrara before the antique statue of Hercules, Bonfini just offering his book, with Galeotto Marzio and Ransanus. The Hungarian members of Matthias' court stand on the left. János Vitéz can be identified by his cardinal's garment and the deed of foundation of the *Academia Istropolitana* of Pozsony (Bratislava), Janus Pannonius by his lilac-coloured frock, while Tamás Bakócz's profile appears in the background. The left-hand side of the foreground is occupied by Baron Péter Apor, the author of *Metamorphosis Transylvaniae* and István Beythe, the first scholar of botany. The painter's initials and the date are in the bottom left-hand side corner: K. Lotz, 1891.

The left-hand side section of the triptych depicts the most important personalities of the Reformation and the Counter-Reformation, with Péter Pázmány in the centre. Miklós Telegdy, bishop of Pécs, and György Káldy, the Jesuit translator of the Bible, stand behind him to the right. The figure of István Verbőczy, a jurist, is on the right-hand side, turning to the right. He wears a yellow dolman and a blue pelisse. Ferenc Forgách, the bishop of Várad, and a historiographer, sits beside him; while the historian, Antal Verancsics, and Miklós Istvánffy stand on the platform. Gáspár Károli, the Protestant Bible translator, sits on the stairs absorbed in his book. The artist, or rather, the commissioners of the work, chose the members of the left-hand side group from among the leading personalities of the Reformation: Ferenc Dávid, János Erdősi Sylvester, István Gelei Katona, Péter Alvinczy and János Czeglédy. Lotz must have been faced with the greatest difficulty here, as hardly any reliable portraits of the above people have been left to us. Gábor Bethlen, Prince of Transylvania, and Zsuzsanna Lórántffy are on the gallery with János Kemény and Gáspár Heltai behind them.

The dominant figure on the right-hand side painting is Miklós Zrínyi, the poet and general. The poets János Gyöngyössy and László Listius can be recognized behind him. The Baroque literature of Hungary is represented by ruling prince Ferenc Rákóczi II, Kelemen Mikes, János Rimai and Ferenc Faludy on the right, and János Haller, Dávid Rozsnyai and Péter Ilosvai Selymes on the left. The painted gallery here, too, becomes populated. Mihály Sztáray holds a sealed diploma; Mária Széchy, the Venus of Murány, can be found by following the direction of Gyöngyössy's eye. Besides them, Sándor Felvinczy and Mrs. Lőrinc Pekri née Kata Szidónia Petrőczy, a poetess, are also on the gallery. Bálint Balassi, the outstanding Renaissance poet, moves down the stairs turning his back to Zrínyi; Sebestyén Tinódi Lantos, a bard of Hungary's 16th century history, is seated on the left of the platform.

Károly Lotz broke with the traditions of monumental Baroque painting by omitting heavenly elements from his compositions. His ideal was Raffaello, who, on the Parnasse of the Stanza della Segnatura in the Vatican, portrayed historical figures in an idealized tableau, that is, he grouped them in a way they never appeared together. Lotz's commissioners expected him to introduce the outstanding figures of Hungary's cultural and literary history. This, especially in the medieval part, was practically impossible because of the lack of representative writer-personalities, who could be portrayed by individual features. Therefore he chose to characterize each era by the ruling monarch, and placed the representatives of literature in his retinue. He had to depict the historical figures portrayed in his pictures as they were generally known at the end of the 19th century, not, however, in an epic form, in action, but statically, in a situation corresponding to their historical significance and personality. In the age of historism it was not inconsistent with the idealized concept of history for persons distant in space or time to appear together in the paintings (e.g. Coloman Beauclerc of the 12th, and Pelbárt Temesvári of the 15th century etc.). The relationship between the figures of the compositions is, as a consequence, merely formal.

Mór Than (1828—1899) painted several of the same themes on the frieze of the National Museum's staircase in 1876 as Lotz in the Academy. Although Than did not have such abundant means of artistic expression at his command as Lotz did, who, among others, worked with him in the Museum as well, he used fewer figures in his compositions, and on several occasions his graphic and pictorial solutions also left something to be desired, nevertheless, as far as ideological unity is concerned, he created something superior to the paintings of the Academy.

The formal solution of the frescoes proves Lotz's outstanding craftsmanship. The harmony of his bright colours unites cheerfully the otherwise unrelated figures and events. The repoussoir-like still-lifes in the foreground increase the depth of space. The same purpose is served by the cleverly distributed shadows, falling according to the actual positioning of the pictures. The low horizontal line is also a consequence of the actual high position of the paintings. The artist found the proper balance between illusion of reality and decorative simplification. The composition, later both in respect of its subject and its origin, is even lighter and more picturesque.

Lotz painted the allegory of Science and Poetry on the ceiling of the Assembly Hall in two octagonal frames. Science is represented by a veiled female figure writing in a book, accompanied by a genius with a torch. Poetry is symbolized by a winged, rising figure holding a lute, followed by Amor and Psyche, the personnifiers of inspiration.

In the five lunettes above the windows Lotz painted, over and above his commission and free of charge, the allegorical representatives of the five classes of the Academy in a form similar to Michelangelo's Sybillas in the Sistine Chapel. The chief figure of each composition is a women seated, embodying a main discipline, while the monochrome subordinate characters refer to related disciplines. Proceeding left to right they follow in this sequence:

1. The main figure, Natural Science, accompanied by Chemistry and Physics.
2. Mathematics with Astronomy and Geography.
3. Literature, that is, Epic Poetry with Lyrical Poetry and Drama.
4. Clio, representing Historiography, with Archaeology and Philology.
5. The main figure of Law and Political Science accompanied by Diplomatics and Rhetorics.

*

Turning to the left on the first floor we arrive at the Presidium and the Scientists' Club. The paintings and sculptures exhibited in the *Presidential Secretariat* are as follows: the portraits of Lóránd Eötvös by Gyula Benczur, László Szalay by Bertalan Székely, Mihály Vörösmarty by Miklós Barabás (1810—1898), Ferenc Kazinczy by Josef Kreutzinger (1757—1829), Imre Madách by Ignác Roskovics, Miklós Wesselényi and Zsigmond Kemény both by Miklós Barabás, Károly Kisfaludy (a copy), the bronze bust of Zoltán Kodály by Gyula Palotai and the marble bust of Frigyes Korányi. The portrait of Ferenc Kazinczy, leading writer of the Hungarian Age of Enlightenment, painted by the Viennese Josef Kreutzinger, is the most outstanding piece in the Hungarian writer's iconography. By omitting superfluous details, the painter, helped by light-effects, directs the observer's attention to the intelligent face. The neutral background and the clothing, painted with delicate strokes of the brush, serve to bring into relief the face as the mirror of character. Vörösmarty's portrait by Barabás also belongs among the treasures of the iconography of Hungarian literary history. It was commissioned by the members of the Aurora Circle to help the young painter, who moved to Pest only recently. Beyond that it also proves the contemporary popularity of the author of "Szózat", the second Hungarian National Anthem. Bertalan Székely was a leading representative of the Academic-style historical painting. Besides his monumental composition he left behind some outstanding portraits as well, among others the portrait of László Szalay, secretary-general of the Academy and a renowned jurist and historian. The nobility of the posture indicates his social position, the huge books and documents, arranged in an attribute-like manner, refer to his profession.

The rooms of the *Scientists' Club* were partly furnished with old furniture, the glass cabinets exhibit relics from the Academy's collections. The walls are decorated with paintings and a few tapestries. From the former we will mention those related to the history of the institution: Ferenc Toldy's portrait by György Vastagh (1834—1922), Farkas Bolyai's portrait (copy), a handsome oil painting of an unknown man incorrectly identified as Sándor Kisfaludy, the contemporary portrait of Mrs. Ferenc Kazinczy, Ferenc Kölcsey's portrait by Anton Einsle (1801—1871), the portrait of the old Ferenc Kazinczy by Johann Ender (1793—1854), Alajos Mednyánszky's portrait by Ferenc Simó (1801—1869), the portraits of Miklós Jósika and András Fáy by an unknown master, Sándor Kisfaludy by Simó, Mihály Esterházy by Johann Ender, István Széchenyi by Miklós Barabás, Aurél Dessewffy by an unknown master, Sámuel Fabriczy by József Czauczig (1781—

26

1857), György Károlyi and Ábrahám Vay by Johann Ender (it must be noted here that the captions of the Vay and Esterházy portraits were exchanged by mistake), János Imre by Johann Ender, a portrait of the young István Széchenyi with a gun across his shoulder by Johann Ender, Sándor Petőfi in his study by Soma Orlai Petrich (1822—1880), Dániel Berzsenyi and the protrait of a woman by Miklós Barabás, Kazinczy's birthplace and grave by Károly Jakobey (1825—1891), two seascapes by Károly Kisfaludy (1788—1830), István Széchenyi by Mór Than, the portrait of the infant Ferenc Rákóczi II, the children of János Podmaniczky by Ádám Mányoki (1673—1757). In the last room hangs a coloured ink drawing by Mihály Zichy (1827—1906), entitled "Music accompanies you from the cradle to the grave", originally a sketch for the frieze of a concert hall, from the legacy of Géza Voinovich. The strip-like composition was put on a scroll, thus, when opened out, the sequence of scenes is reversed. The portrait of János Arany by Mihály Kovács (1818—1892) can be seen in the same room.

Johann Ender accompanied István Széchenyi on his journey to the Orient. The watercolour, showing the young aristocrat in an informal posture, may have been painted during this journey. The mannered deportment and attire serve the portrayal of character, introducing a man who conducts his life on a large scale according to his own rules. The Transylvanian Ferenc Simó depicts Sándor Kisfaludy as the already famous poet, although the accessories of his profession are not present in the painting. The patch of the intelligent face is set off by the dark, braided clothing suggesting a noble origin, and the clouded sky. The fact that the painting was soon reproduced from copper plate proves its popularity.

The Viennese Anton Einsle was often commissioned by Hungarians. The portrait of Ferenc Kölcsey, author of the National Anthem, is one of his most important, Hungarian-related paintings. Soma Orlai Petrich's place in the history of art is among the pioneers of Hungarian historical painting, but he also left some outstanding portraits behind. All his life he was preoccupied by the figure of Sándor Petőfi, his distant relative and good friend. His painting, which depicts Petőfi at his desk, is so close to the half-length portrait of the poet, dated 1848 and kept in the National Museum, that it must have come into being soon afterwards.

If, reaching the first floor, we turn to the right, we come to the Secretary-general's office, the Lecture Hall, the Hall of Pictures and the Presidential Conference Room. In the rooms of the Secretary-general's office a memorial tablet deserves to be mentioned commemorating Béla Bartók's activities in the arrangement of folksongs which took place in the building 1934—1940.

27

The stucco ornaments of the *Lecture Hall* are by János Marschalkó. Earlier inscriptions, concerning the disciplines of the Academy, have disappeared from the spandrels. In 1871 four idealized landscape scenes by the late-romantic Antal Ligeti (1823–1890) were fitted into the narrower walls of the hall. These are: The Fortresses of Trencsén (now Trenčin) and Szigliget, Szepesvár (Spišski Hrad) and Hricsó (Hričov). Besides these four paintings the room is decorated by statues: Zsigmond Kemény by Alajos Stróbl, Károly Kisfaludy by György Kiss (1852–1916 or 1919) Ferenc Kazinczy (copied from István Ferenczy's original by János Marschalkó), József Eötvös by Miklós Vay (1828–1886), Pál Gyulai by Alajos Stróbl, István Széchenyi copied from the Viennese Hans Gasser's (1817–1868) original. Gasser's was, by the way, the only statue which István Széchenyi posed for. A marble bust of János Balassa is also in the hall; that of Sándor Kőrösi Csoma by Barnabás Holló is exhibited in the corridor partitioned off the hall after World War II.

The *Hall of Pictures* houses five paintings and two statues: the portraits of Géza Kuun by Aladár Edvi Illés (1870–1958), Ferenc Deák by Mór Than, the busts of Gergely Csiky by György Zala (1858–1937) and that of Miklós Jósika by Alajos Stróbl. The portrait of István Széchenyi was ordered by his two brothers, Lajos and Pál, in 1836 from a representative of Viennese Biedermeier portrait painter, Friedrich von Amerling (1803–1887). The composition belongs to Amerling's most monumental works. The wish of the donors was, according to the deed of gift: "if only our future great grandchildren, looking upon the features of this picture, were inspired to the sentiments of this noblest heart, and be roused to the greatest deeds for the good of their country and nation." The large portrait of József Eötvös, exhibited here as a deposit from the National Museum, is the work of Viktor Madarász (1830–1917). Madarász was an outstanding historical- and portrait painter. Although with this picture he had to make concessions to the commissioners' requirements concerning what they regarded to be a representative portrait, he still succeeded, in front of a background crammed with accessories to express the character of his subject. Johann Ender's huge oil painting depicting the allegory of the Academy hangs by the door. In the composition Hebe offers a drink from her cup to Jupiter's eagle. Both this scene and the relief on the shield of the female figure with an idealized face refers to the advancement of the Hungarian world of science. On the relief, after Raffaello, Attila refrains from destroying Rome at the intervention of Pope Leo. Ender's model was a similar painting by John Hoppner, noticed perhaps by István Széchenyi during the course of his travels in England, possibly through the medium of a copperplate reproduction.

A number of paintings hang on the wall of the corridor leading to the Presidential Conference Room: Győző Concha and Pál Gyulai by Ede Balló, Jenő Balogh by Oszkár Glatz (1872—1958), Géza Mihalovich by Andor Boruth, László Szalay by Bertalan Székely, Lőrinc Tóth by József Prohászka (1885—1964), Kálmán Thaly, Gusztáv Heinrich, Albin Csáky and Sámuel Brassai all four by Andor Boruth, Árpád Berczik by Menyhért Both (1857—1916), György Volf by Antal Zilzer (1860—1921), András Fáy by Miklós Barabás, József Dessewffy (a copy), Aurél Ignác Fessler by János Rombauer (1782—1849), Gyula Pauler by Imre Révész (1859—1945), Miklós Jósika by Lajos Ábrányi (1849—1901), Ferenc Deák by Miklós Barabás, Gábor Döbrentei by Mihály Kovács, Farkas Bolyai by Lajos Thanhoffer (1843—1909), and Lajos Lóczy by Antal Meggyesi Schwartz. János Rombauer of Lőcse worked in Northern Hungary but meanwhile spent almost 20 years in Russia. There he met with the famous historian, Aurél Ignác Fessler, whose portrait he painted and brought back home with him. This brilliant portrait is one of the masterpieces in Rombauer's oeuvre.

The paintings decorating the *Presidential Conference Room* are the following: Endre Hőgyes by Jenő Jandrassik (1860—1919), Ferenc Bene by Lajos Györgyi-Giergl (1821—1863), Kálmán Mikszáth by Endre Komáromi-Kacz (1880—1969), Mihály Horváth by Nándor Rákosi (1832—1884), Lajos Ilosvai by Károly Lotz, József Eötvös by Bertalan Székely, Gyula Kautz by György Vastagh, Károly Than by Ede Balló, József Budenz by Aladár Körösfői-Kriesch (1863—1920), Pál Hunfalvy by Géza Biczó, Lajos Markusovszky by Jenő Jendrassik, János Arany by Miklós Barabás, Károly Kisfaludy (a copy), Mór Jókai (Ede Balló's copy after the original by Lipót Horovitz), Petőfi in Debrecen by Soma Orlai Petrich, Pál Szemere and Pál Almási Balogh by Mihály Kovács, Béla Fogarasi by Heinrich Vogeler (1872—1942), Károly Szász by Andor Boruth, Gábor Szarvas by Antal Zilzer, Frigyes Korányi, Sándor Korányi and Zsolt Beöthy, all three by Ede Balló, and Géza Entz by Antal Meggyesi Schwartz.

V. THE SECOND FLOOR

The design of the staircase leading up to the second floor is similar to that used a floor below. The two ends of its middle section are decorated by gold-plated cast-iron candelabra on imitation marble pedestals. The marble bust of György Bessenyei by Ede Kallós (1866–1950) stand on the landing on the second floor. Since no reliable portrait of the guardsman-writer is existent, the authenticity of the bust is questionable. The rosetted archivolts with braided-ribbon patterns between the five semicircular-arched windows are supported by arabesque-decorated half-pillars. The plaster statues and reliefs decorating the pillars were cast by János Marschalkó after models imported from Berlin.

*

To the right on the second floor we find the Small and the Large conference rooms. Both were designed by Dr. Iván Kocsis, whose plans were also followed when the Lecture Hall was remodelled. To the left we find the offices of the Library Directorate. Three paintings can be seen there: the portrait of Ferenc Toldy by Mihály Kovács, József Teleki by Miklós Barabás and Kálmán Mikszáth by Gyula Benczur. In the portrait of the Library's founder, József Teleki, Barabás excelled in the splendid detail of the richly decorated clothing. Gyula Benczúr was the official, well-known portrait painter at the turn of the century. His portrait of Mikszáth, dated 1910, demonstrated his immense professional skill. An interesting point about the portrait is that Benczúr submitted it as his "inauguration address" to the Academy.

The building, over a hundred years old, is no longer able to satisfy the Academy's demand for space, growing in proportion to the institution's increasing tasks. The institution outgrew its home: the majority of the Academy's official apparatus is already working outside the building. But the building is still worthy of our respect as a monument to the Academy's heroic past and a monumental document of one of the periods in the architectural history of Budapest. The vestibule, the staircase and the Assembly Hall comprise a remarkable ensemble even today. It provides a distinguished, befitting framework for the most important, representative events of the Academy.

*

The third floor of the building often played a part in the history of the Academy; its rooms with their overhead lighting, are pre-eminently suitable for exhibitions of pictures. Unfortunately, because of technical problems, the third floor cannot fulfil this function.

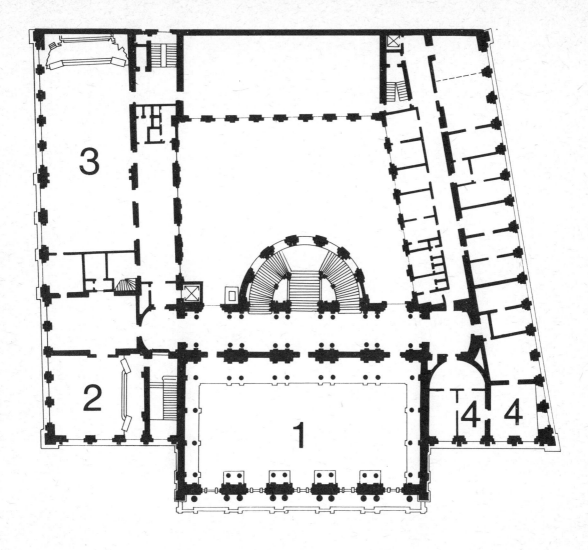

Second floor plan
1. Assembly Hall. 2. Small Conference Room. 3. Large Conference Room. 4. Library Directorate.

SELECTED BIBLIOGRAPHY

DIVALD Kornél: A Magyar Tudományos Akadémia palotája és gyűjteményei. Magyarázó kalauz. Bp. 1917. MTA. 143 p. [The Palace and Collections of the Hungarian Academy of Sciences. A Vade Mécum]

HENSZLMANN Imre: Az Akadémia palotájának eddigi története. = Kritikai Lapok, 1. 1862. 10–23. p. [The History of the Palace of the Academy to date]

Emlékkönyv a Magyar Akadémia palotájának megnyitási ünnepélyére. Pest, 1865. Deutsch. 24 p. 9 t. [Memorial Volume for the Inauguration Ceremony of the Hungarian Academy]

BERZEVICZY Albert: Az Akadémia palotájának félszázados fennállása. = Budapesti Szemle, 162. 1915. 321–328. p. [The Golden Jubilee of the Palace of the Academy]

FRÁTER Zsuzsa: „Nemzeti részvét emelte". 100 évvel ezelőtt kezdték építeni az Akadémia palotáját. = Magyar Tudomány, 7. 1962. 6–7. 450–459. p. [„Raised by the Nation". Building of the Palace of the Academy Commenced 100 Years ago]

KOMÁRIK, Dénes: Der Bau des Palastes der Akademie von Pest. = Die ungarische Kunstgeschichte und die Wiener Schule 1846–1930. Ausstellungskatalog Wien, Collegium Hungaricum. Budapest, 1983. 25–28. p.

YBL Ervin: A Magyar Tudományos Akadémia falképei. = YBL Ervin: Lotz Károly élete és művészete. Bp. 1938. MTA. 245–265. p., 484–489. p. [The Wall-paintings of the Hungarian Academy of Sciences. In: YBL, Ervin: The Life and Art of Károly Lotz]

KŐSZEGI László: Az Akadémia dísztermének Lotz-falképei. = Képzőművészet, 7. 1933. 63–64. p., 165–169. p. [Lotz-frescoes in the Assembly Hall of the Academy]

A díszterem falfestményei. = Akadémiai Értesítő, 1892. 263–266. p. [The Frescoes of the Assembly Hall]

SZÉPHELYI FRANKL, György: Das Bildprogramm des Festsaals der Ungarischen Akademie der Wissenschaften. = Die ungarische Kunstgeschichte und die Wiener Schule 1846–1930. Ausstellungskatalog Wien, Collegium Hungaricum. Budapest, 1983. 56–62. p.

VISZOTA Gyula: A Magyar Tudományos Akadémia címere. = Akadémiai Értesítő, 15. 1904. 5—11. p. [The Coat of Arms of the Hungarian Academy of Sciences]

RÓZSA György: Die Allegorie der Ungarischen Akademie der Wissenschaften — Johann Ender und István Széchenyi. = Alte und Moderne Kunst, 11. 1966. 88. 28—31. p.

PULSZKY Károly: Az Akadémia szerepe a képzőművészetek fejlesztésében. = Akadémiai Értesítő, 1892. 333—340. p. [The Role of the Academy in the Development of Visual Arts]

A M. Tud. Akadémia képesterme. = Akadémiai Értesítő, 1891. 32—35. p., 663—667. p. [The Hall of Pictures in the Hungarian Academy of Sciences]

The Library of the Hungarian Academy of Sciences 1826—1976. Ed. by György Rózsa etc. Bp. 1976. MTAK. 40 p. 36 t.

A Magyar Tudományos Akadémia másfél évszázada 1825—1975. Főszerk. Pach Zsigmond Pál. Szerk. Vörös Antal. Bp. 1975. Akad. K. 548 p. [150 Years of the Hungarian Academy of Sciences 1825—1975]

LIST OF PHOTOGRAPHS

1. The Pest side bridge head of the Chain Bridge before the construction. Detail from R. Alt's lithography
2. The completed building with Coronation Hill in front. Photo by Gy. Klösz
3. Henszlmann's design. Wood engraving
4. Ferstel's design. Wood engraving
5. Skalnitzky's design. Wood engraving
6. Klenze's design. Wood engraving
7. Stüler's design. Wood engraving
8. The National Museum of Stockholm by Stüler
9. The main facade
10. View of the building from Chain Bridge
11. View of the building with the Buda hills in the background
12. A committee session of the House of Representatives in Committee in the Assembly Hall. Wood engraving, 1865
13. The Esterházy Gallery on the third floor. Wood engraving, 1874
14. The exhibition of the Historical Picture Gallery on the third floor. 1920s
15. The relief by Barnabás Holló on the Akadémia Street side
16. The Lecture Hall after World War II
17. The Library's Catalogue Room
18. The Library's Reading Room
19. The old stacks area
20. The Reading Room of the Oriental Collection
21. The Collection of Manuscripts
22. The Assembly Hall
23. The Assembly Hall and its frescoes on the Danube side
24. The age of King Coloman. Detail from Károly Lotz's fresco
25. The age of Stephen I. Detail from Károly Lotz's fresco

Cover: Adam Slowikowski's coloured lithography from the middle 1860s. — The description of paintings and sculptures was based on conditions in 1982. When more than one painting is in a room, the description proceeds from left to right.

Sources of photographs:

The Photographic Archives of the Academy's Library: Nos. 3–7, 12, 17, 19, 23, 33, 36–37, 40, 43–47, 49–50
Hungarian National Museum: cover, and Nos. 1, 13, 24–26, 28–30, 34–35, 38–39, 41–42
MTI, the Hungarian Telegraphic Agency: Nos. 10–11, 15, 18, 20–21, 31, 48
National Inspectorate for Architectural Monuments: Nos. 9, 14, 22, 27, 32
Budapest Historical Museum: No. 2
Stockholm, Nationalmuseum: No. 8
Mr. Pál Gergely: No. 16

Felelős kiadó: az MTA Könyvtár főigazgatója
Alak BN/12 – Terjedelem: 10 (A/5) ív
Megjelent: 1984 – Példányszám: 3000
Készült az MTA Sokszorosítójában 8314389
F. v.: dr. Héczey Lászlóné

PHOTOGRAPHS

1

3

4

5

6

7

8

9

10

11

12

14

15

16

17

18

19

20

21

22

23

24

25

26

27

28

29

30

32

33

34

35

36

37

38

40

41

42

43

44

45

46

50